The Best Kids Explore Central Florida © 2021 by Joshua Best

Contact the publisher:
Unprecedented Press LLC - 229 W Main Ave, Zeeland, MI 49464
www.unprecedentedpress.com | info@unprecedentedpress.com
instagram: unprecedentedpress

ISBN: 978-1-7321964-8-3

Ingram Printing & Distribution, 2021

First Edition

Unprecedented Press

the
BEST KIDS
explore

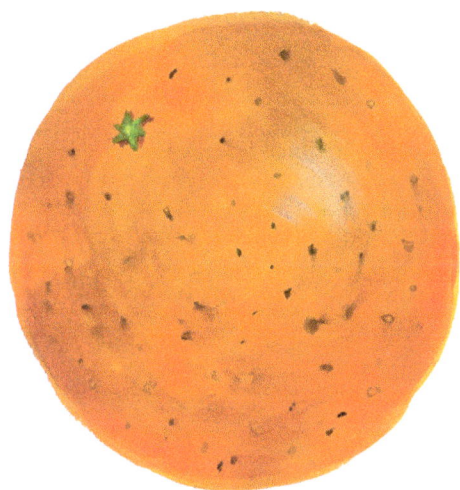

CENTRAL
FLORIDA

CONTENTS

FLORIDA

Tallahassee

Jacksonville

Cocoa Beach

Orlando

Winter Garden

Lake Buena Vista

Tampa

Major City

Capital City

Story Location

Miami

MEET THE KIDS

Exploring is the best. Exploring lets you discover the cool things around you - things you didn't know were there before. That's what makes it so much fun! It's exciting to find out what's around the corner, across the border and beyond the horizon.

The Best kids are explorers. They love finding new places to play and discovering new ways to have fun. The oldest one is Frederick – he has orange hair. The middle one is Edith – she has brown hair. The youngest is Hugo – he has yellow hair. The Best kids are half American and half Canadian. They live in Michigan.

In this book, the kids travel to the state of Florida. At the time of their expedition, Frederick was six years old, Edith was four years old, and Hugo was one year old. This trip occurred in the month of February.

LODGING & TRANSPORT

With Hugo just over a year old, the best family decided that flying was the best way to get to Central Florida. It meant shorter travel times, and it seemed wise to take advantage of the free flight (kids under two fly for free by sitting on a parent's lap).

The kids' dad was able to find a direct flight on a Denver-based airline called Frontier, which departed from their hometown in Michigan and arrived at MCO airport in Orlando.

For this trip, they rented a midsize sedan from the Thrifty car rental office at the Orlando airport. Along with the rental, they reserved one car seat and two booster seats. Since they were only staying five nights, and the kids weren't very big, it was the perfect size.

THE GROVE
RESORT &
SUITES

For lodging in central Florida, the Best family chose a
location that was filled with amenities and activities,
so they wouldn't have to go very far to have fun. They
booked a two bedroom suite at a resort called The Grove
Resort & Suites. It was well situated in Winter Garden
(near Disney World), and it featured a pool, waterslide,
lazy river and arcade room. The multiple bedroom suite
was a game changer for this young family whose kids
had different bedtimes. Their favorite parts of the room
included the balcony, and the TV in the kids' bedroom.
Their mom and dad liked the full kitchen, so they could
make healthy, affordable meals.

APPLES AND ORANGES

t was gray in Michigan. The snow on the ground was turning brown and the Best kids hadn't seen the sun in weeks.

"Beep, beep, beep."

Frederick's alarm clock went off bright and early. He peeled back his grey woolen blanket and jumped out of bed. Today was the day they were going to Florida.

"Get up, get up!" Frederick yelled throughout the house. Edith yawned and Hugo popped his head above the top bar of his crib.

Downstairs, their mom and dad were packing lunches and putting bags into the car. Each of the kids had their own backpack filled with toys and art supplies for the journey ahead.

Once they arrived at the airport, the kids got really excited. This was their first time flying on an

airplane. From the window at the gate, they could see the plane being filled up with luggage. It was huge! It had big, green letters across the side, huge wings with engines underneath, and a picture of a bright orange fox printed on the tail.

"Wow!" said Edith.

"Whoa!" said Hugo.

The kids boarded the plane, buckled their seatbelts and immediately asked their parents for a snack. Their mom reached in her bag and handed them each a small tin filled with apple slices. They were the crispy kind. They tasted like home.

After waiting for nearly an hour, the plane began to move and finally took off into the air. The jolt pushed Frederick against the back of the seat. He laughed at the feeling. The tilt of the airplane flying upward caused Edith to open her eyes very wide. She was a little nervous. Hugo was perched on his dad's lap, trying not to squirm.

The airplane landed in the city of Orlando in North-central Florida. Everything was instantly different. Instead of gray and brown, plants were green.

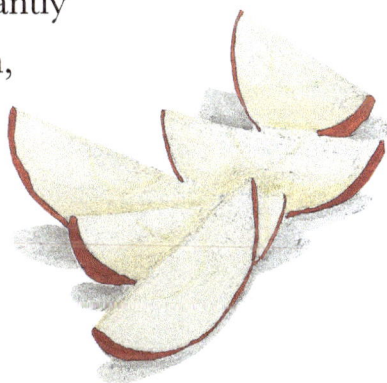

"Look!" said Frederick.
"A palm tree!"

Everyone turned and gazed with wonder. "Look!" said their dad, "orange trees!"

The view out the left side of the car was lush. The trees were lined perfectly row by row, and speckled with orange dots. The air was warm and smelled fresh.

Frederick, Edith, and Hugo settled in and unpacked their things when they arrived at the resort − another first for the Bests. It was evening now, and after popping out for some groceries, their dad returned with a bundle of local Florida oranges. It was hard to wait until after dinner to slice open the juicy citrus fruit.

When it was finally time to cut into the oranges, the family migrated to their balcony on the fifth floor and looked out across the southern woods. The sky was full of color. Vibrant tangerine and violet light was making the clouds glow in front of their eyes. As orange juice dripped off their chins, the winter blues began to fade away. And they all wondered if this was the official taste of sunshine.

COUSINS WITH CANNONS

The Best kids' mom and dad woke up to the sound of toy cars sliding across the floor in the living room. It was a nice place; it had two separate bedrooms, a kitchen and a living room with a balcony. The kids had awoken early because they were so excited to explore the resort.

Before breakfast was served, Frederick opened the sliding door and walked onto the balcony. This was the moment he remembered the resort had a waterpark! The first thing that caught his eye was the giant waterslide. It was green and orange with all sorts of twists and turns. Instantly he blurted,

"Can we go down the waterslide?!?"

His parents looked at each other and nodded their heads. His mom said, "Let's go down there for a swim with Lucy and Anna this morning."

Lucy and Anna were the Best kids' cousins from Canada. They were also visiting Florida, and they got a room in the same resort, just four doors down the hall.

The kids quickly put their swimsuits on along with their sandals, hats and sunblock. Edith wore a swimsuit with snazzy pink frills, Frederick wore a hat with a shark on the front, and Hugo looked like a little orange marshmallow with his new swimmies.

Finally, they met up with their aunt, uncle and cousins in the hallway, and walked down the stairs towards the waterpark. When they found the perfect spot, they laid their towels and sandals by the sun loungers. Frederick immediately asked to go on the waterslide and his dad agreed to go with him to check it out.

As they climbed up numerous sets of stairs and looked down on the rest of the park, they felt squeamish inside. It was a long way down! At the top, there was a lifeguard with a stick. She held it up beside Frederick and frowned. It was a few inches taller than he was.

"I'm sorry," she said. "You have to be this tall to go down the slide."

Feeling sad, Frederick and his dad walked back down the stairs.

"I'm sorry that you can't go down the slide, but let's try the lazy river. We can bring everyone along."

Frederick didn't like the idea of a lazy river. He didn't think it looked like much fun, but he agreed to go.

Edith, her cousin Lucy, and her aunt Sarah were the first ones to reach the starting point of the lazy river. It was filled with yellow, inflated tubes for you to sit in and drift along with. As they entered the water, they realized, it wasn't boring at all! In fact, the water had such a strong current, that it swept you up and pushed you along. The girls laughed and giggled as they tried to grab onto a tube without being swept away. A little further behind, was the rest of the crew: mom, dad, Frederick, Hugo, uncle Luke and cousin Anna.

They had the same experience as they tried hard to get into a tube before the water pushed them too far. Frederick's frown disappeared as he felt the rush of the waves.

As the second group approached the halfway mark in the river, they found Lucy and Edith waiting for them around a bend – except they weren't in the river anymore. They were on a bridge over top of the river spraying water on the others! As jet streams of water shot from the yellow water cannons above and hit the rest of the family below, the girls laughed and gave each other a high five.

Mom and Frederick were the most clever tube riders. They flipped their tubes over and used them as shields from the spray. Hugo sat on his dad's lap in a tube and Anna sat in Uncle Luke's lap while they pushed off from the edges, and spun their tubes around to avoid the blast (without success). But as Frederick avoided the cannons and dodged the spray, a big grin appeared on his face. This was way more fun than going down a slide.

DINNER WITH DINOS

As a young family on a budget, the Bests decided it wasn't quite time for the full Walt Disney World theme park experience, so the team decided to test the waters. Together with their cousins, aunt and uncle, they drove to Disney springs for an afternoon of shopping and to have some dinner.

Driving onto the Disney campus was like traveling to another country. They had their own buses, their own hotels, and their own street signs! Their crew of nine (extended family included) finally found parking close together. There were so many parking lots, they had to be organized by color and number. The Best kids parked in section Green 35.

Snap, snap, snap. Out came the collapsible travel strollers for little Hugo and cousin Anna. Before they could say, "Mickey Mouse!" the team was going down the escalator that opened into the facility. The first thing they did was find a map and chart their course through the friendly neighborhood.

It was fun to browse around shops and stroll down the brick roads, but nothing could beat their experience at The Disney Store because their parents said they could buy a souvenir. It was a big building that was separated into departments based on different Disney movies. At first, everyone walked through the section of classic characters – Mickey, Minnie, Donald, Goofy and Pluto. You could buy anything imaginable with mouse ears attached.

Next, there was a princess section, and then a hero section with Marvel toys and clothes. At the very back, was Frederick's favorite - the Star Wars department. After looking through

every single object, and knowing he could only spend $10, Frederick chose a Darth Maul and a Darth Vader Hot Wheels car. Edith picked a tiara that matched Princess Elena of Avalor's. Hugo chose a colorful tin of Disney-themed mints with Mickey Mouse on the outside.

As afternoon turned into evening, the Best kids and their cousins needed to find a place to eat supper. Frederick's tummy started rumbling.

"I'm so hungry, I could eat a zebra!" he exclaimed.

Uncle Luke laughed because he remembered Simba said the same thing in one of his favorite Disney movies.

"I don't think that's your tummy roaring, Frederick," said Aunt Sarah. "Turn around! We've arrived at the dinosaur restaurant!"

When Frederick looked up, he saw the entrance to the T-Rex Cafe. Inside, reptilian colors flashed and loud roars boomed. Beside the entrance, he noticed that Edith was already climbing on a dinosaur skeleton.

"Is this where we're going to eat?" asked cousin Lucy.

"You bet!" said her dad.

The first thing they noticed when they walked inside was a gigantic, purple Tyrannosaurus Rex towering overhead. It was pretty scary!

When it was time for them to be seated, the server brought them through the restaurant. It looked like the inside of a prehistoric cave. Flashes of orange light were illuminating one corner of the room, and orbs of blue light were glowing on the other side. Finally, they sat down to eat only to realize there was a robotic Triceratops standing right over their table.

"Aaaaah!" Anna screamed.

"I scared." said Hugo.

Once they got over their fears, the restaurant turned out to be super cool and the food was good too.

At their giant circular table, they laughed, played with their toys, colored with crayons, and filled their tummies to the brim. When they finished chowing down their dinner, the massive table was covered with crumbs, messy plates, empty cups, spilled condiments, melted ice cubes, scrunched up napkins, and broken crayons. That's when they realized five kids can make a dino-sized mess!

THE COCOA CUP

One morning in Central Florida, the Best family switched on the TV to check the weather for the day ahead. A nice man with a fancy, orange tie was giving the weather report. He announced this would be the nicest day of the week. That's when mom's ears perked up. She was excited to spend a day outside in nature, so they decided this was it! And they went to the beach.

Cocoa Beach is sixty miles due east of Orlando. It sits on Florida's east coast near Cape Canaveral (where space shuttles are launched into orbit). For this reason, some people call this area of Florida the *Space Coast*.

Frederick, Edith, and Hugo squeezed into the backseat of the red Mazda they were renting for the week. They drove under the resort's palm tree canopy, past the orange groves and onto a one lane, rural highway surrounded by happy, green trees.

They turned up the music and sang along to "One Wild Life" by Gungor, as the sun pierced through the clouds

with confidence and hope. The view down the oddly straight road was glorious. It was Sunday morning, and the drive to Cocoa Beach filled their souls with joy, as if they were singing in church.

They began the day at Lori Wilson Park, a public access point to Cocoa Beach, where the kids faced their first challenge.

Frederick was so excited for the beach that he didn't want to wait in line (it was pretty long) to use the change rooms provided, so his dad suggested changing in the open while he blocked everyone's view with a towel. A frightened look came on over Frederick's face. This was a pretty busy beach, so putting on his swimsuit in the open air didn't seem safe, but his Dad assured him he would block everyone from seeing, and that he too would look away. Frederick took a deep breath and went for it.

Between a section of oceanside bushes and a shark-print towel, Frederick got dressed and was ready in record time. He met the challenge.

"That was easy!" Frederick exclaimed, as he raced past his siblings who were waiting in line with their mother. Down the boardwalk he went, out to the Atlantic Ocean. It was the the first act of bravery at Cocoa Beach that day.

Once they were all out on the sand together, the sun perked up and everyone was happy to be outside. After getting the ocean swimming safety lesson from dad, Frederick and Edith ran straight toward the water, and began to splash and swim. Being from Michigan, the Best kids were used to the freshwater of the Great Lakes. In fact, this was the first time they ever swam in salt water. When their parents explained the difference, they encouraged the kids to taste the water, but not to drink it. The older two kids tried it and immediately spit it out. It was Hugo's turn to give it a shot, but he was scared after seeing Frederick's and Edith's reactions.

"You got this, buddy!" they cheered.

Mustering the courage, he scooped water into his hand
and touched his tongue to it. He immediately squinted
his eyes and squished up his face. Then, he started
laughing, and the
others joined. It was
the second act of
bravery at Cocoa
Beach that day.

ON COCOA BEACH:
"I liked getting the shees...seas...
seashells. Ah! It's hard to say!"

After they swam,
played in the sand,
collected seashells, relaxed in the sun and gathered their
towels, the Best family headed down the beach to a
restaurant with a beachside patio. It had a chill vibe, tiki
decorations, and a statue of a pirate! The kids ordered
hot dogs and chicken strips, their mom ordered a salad,
but their dad wanted seafood.

"We're at the ocean! I've gotta have seafood!" he insisted.
So, he ordered a platter of fried calamari, which is
another word for squid.

When the dish arrived, dad took a piece of calamari and dipped it in the marinara sauce they were served with.

"Yum! These are good!" he proclaimed.

Then their dad asked around the table if anyone wanted to try some calamari. Mom agreed, but Frederick shook his head. Hugo said, "No thanks!" and at first, Edith also declined.

"Are you sure?" asked her dad.

Edith looked around the table, and decided to seize her moment. "Okay, I'll try it." she said.

Edith grabbed a piece of fried calamari, dipped it in the red sauce and took a big bite.

"Not bad!" admitted Edith.

This incredible decision was the third act of bravery on Cocoa Beach that day. Each was a contender for the Cocoa Cup, but Edith walked away with the prize. Unfortunately, the prize was just a pat on the back from her family. It wasn't glamorous, but it was a lot of fun!

LITTLE DETAILS

Aside from the sunshine, the best thing about visiting Cocoa Beach was the hunt for seashells. The Best kids' mom and dad let them collect as many as they wanted, but they could only keep three each. It helps make sure there's enough for kids in the future. Here's a sampling of what they came home with.

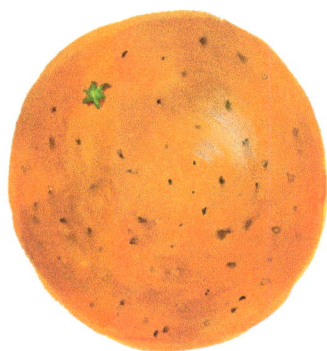

In the first story entitled *Apples and Oranges*, the Best kids' dad brought back some local Florida oranges from the local hispanic supermarket. They were perfectly juicy! Florida is known for growing oranges, grapefruits and other types of citrus fruit.

BEST BETS

THE CRAYOLA EXPERIENCE

One outing that wasn't mentioned in any of the Florida stories, was actually one of the family favorites. The Crayola Experience in Orlando was fun for all three kids, and had something for everyone. Not only can you design your own crayon with a custom paper wrapper, but there is also an indoor playground, a bunch of activities, and a vibrant gift shop. If you're up for a creative afternoon, check this place out!

★★★★★   ★★★★★   ★★★★★

DISNEY SPRINGS

If you're not sure that your kids are quite ready for Disney World, or you're working on a tight budget, try visiting Disney Springs. It's a nice way to dip your toe in the Disney water. There's no entry fee, and you still get to stroll along the well-groomed streets, visit the shops and check out some other cool attractions. You'll end up spending some money, but you'll avoid the ticket charge.

★★★★½   ★★★   ★★★★

BUMPS IN THE ROAD

ONE-YEAR-OLD ON A PLANE

Traveling with young kids can sometimes prove difficult. On this trip, the Best family chose direct flights from their hometown, which made getting to the airport simpler and the flight shorter. Once on the airplane, Hugo struggled to stay seated for the full journey which was approximately three hours long. Since he was under two years old, he was not required to have his own ticket, so on the plus side, it was less expensive. But it also meant he had to sit on his mom or dad's lap throughout the flight. It made him extra squirmy, but it was nothing a couple trips up and down the aisle couldn't mend.

HEIGHT RESTRICTIONS

As mentioned in *Cousins with Cannons*, Frederick was disappointed that he didn't meet the height restriction for the waterslide at Grove Resort. Before traveling anywhere with rides or slides, pull out a tape measure at home and see how much the kids have grown.

CLOUD COVER

If you're planning to visit Central Florida in February, be aware of the fluctuating situation in the sky. This time of year isn't very hot, but if you're from the north, it will be a nice improvement over winter flurries. Specifically, take note that the clouds will come and go, leaving you with an unpredictable day. As they say in Florida, "If you don't like the weather, wait five minutes."

CAR SEATS

Everyone knows that kids need car seats. But not everyone knows that getting car seats from a car rental company can be an expensive add-on. If there are multiple kids in your family, make sure to budget extra for the car seats.

ABOUT THE
AUTHOR

The adventures of the Best kids found on these pages
were chronicled by none other than their own father.
Joshua Best is a writer, designer, and illustrator. By day,
he leads the marketing team at a nonprofit network
of children's hospitals. Of all these roles, there is none
better than being a dad to Frederick, Edith and Hugo.

FOLLOW ALONG

Why wait until the next book is released? You can find out now where the kids are headed next. Follow the kids on Instagram to watch illustration in progress and to see real photos of current trips! Also, check out the website for ways to get in touch.

@thebestkidsexplore

thebestkidsexplore.com